THESE SAINTS ARE STONES

THESE SAINTS ARE STONES

POEMS BY MILLIE TULLIS

SIGNATURE BOOKS | 2026 | SALT LAKE CITY

Join our mail list at www.signaturebooks.com for details on events and related titles we think you'll enjoy.

Design by Jason Francis

FIRST EDITION | 2026

Paperback ISBN: 978-1-56085-533-0
Ebook ISBN: 978-1-56085-511-8

CONTENTS

GOD SEES EVERYTHING

but sees
can't be

the word
for how

God
everythings

in my childhood
He saw all

do you need
a body

to house
a verb

Mormon God
has eyes

pupils
a tiny God

shaped window
for Picture

to crawl
through

I

Root: I want to taste your song, to hear your salt.

—Dayna Patterson, *Dear Ellen, 1863*

AFTER

My first sister was named for the pioneer
who hit a hungry Paiute

in the back of the head with fire
wood. My second sister

named for the pioneer
who nursed her dead

sister's baby on the trail. The baby
who fathered the eleventh prophet.

I was named for the woman
who met Butch Cassidy

and didn't tell the sheriff
for three days.

No one is named
for my grandfather's great grandmother,

a pioneer girl
who married

her mother's husband
at sixteen.

Who delivered him
twelve children.

MARTHA,

I know
some things
about how
you lived
here.

The house was wood
and white.
The cellar filled
with potatoes,
pears, little
apples.

I know the year you married him.

Later, a lean-to collapsed
on two of your babies.

Later, your oldest girl
fell in the fire.

I wrote their names down.

But there is more
I can't see.

PINTO CEMETERY

It is not a ghost town.
There is no town.
It's a place.
There is a sign and a road.

A memory:
I was small when
we drove here. Summer.
The long dirt road in.

My parents offered
five bucks to the child
who found David's grave
first. Then pulled up

to this cemetery. Barely
bigger than our yard.
Do I remember this
day or my parents

telling this joke?
There is no grass.
Just fabric flowers
thin from sun.

A chain link fence.
A flagpole.
No flag.
I do not know

which graves
are graves.
Some markers
only branches

or iron
bars rising
from dirt.
Other headstones

are stone
but illegible. Sand
stone after water.
Wind. Years.

This time
I find Alice
and Thomas first.
Their large grey stone

gives no hint
that she remarried
after he died.
The stone is new.

Replaced maybe
forty years ago.
Someone I must
be related to has

struck six metal poles
in the ground
around their graves.
Connected them

with a chain.
Stuffed plastic
flowers down
each pole.

The dirt is grey
in some places.
Pink then
red. Bouquet

of red. Finger
tip small Coral
Gilia dragging
into October.

ALICE

After all
your deaths,
a granddaughter
interviewed the old neighbor in Pinto.

Reading it is the closest I get to you.

Your neighbor named you
Sister
then your first husband's
last name.
She said that house was yours.

You
ran the family
businesses, cut
deep pockets
in all your skirts
to carry those little
leather bags,
the family cash.

When the bishop came
to settle tithing each year,
you could recall
within a pound of cheese
what you'd paid the church.

You did long division in your head.
You could not write
or read.

Made sure
your Martha could.

PINTO CEMETERY

A year after David married Alice
they had their only child
together.
                    Thomas

                    named
                    after Alice's dead
                    first husband.

                    Thomas
             the baby
was sealed
to Thomas
             the father
                    through her.

                          He was David's
                          son in blood.

                          Not in heaven.

Months after
Thomas' birth,
David married
Alice's daughter.

                    Martha.
                    His eternal wife.

      But Alice's baby
                    Thomas
                    is listed
                    on the back of David
                    and Martha's stone
      under   *Our Children.*

First
I think
Thomas
is buried there
too. But he is far from this
family patch of pale earth.

DAVID DREAMS

of Marthy. As young
as the day he met her.
Ten years old under
a freckled nose.
Ten and showing off
ten long fingers.
Her pink fingernails
lift like petals.
He holds her between
finger and thumb. Again
she says again.

AFTER PINTO CEMETERY

When I call my husband about the graves
it's all clarifying relationships.

Who married
who.   Whose
baby was that?

The names are common
and repeated.

I mix up two babies,
realize the next day.

I crave simple sentences. But
confuse

                              mother
              father   husband
daughter   sister   wife.

HELPMEET

Married less than two years
Alice tells David

you need a wife of your own.

The family record says this.

Alice was sealed to her dead first husband.

Women can be sealed once.
Men many times.

Everyone must be sealed
to enter the kingdom of heaven.

So Alice

who was his wife
was only his wife

for time
not eternity.

I imagine
Martha
nearby

when her mother
says this.

If
her mother
says this.

Doing what sixteen year old
pioneer girls did.

Sewing.
Milking.
Gathering eggs.

Holding the baby,
her half
brother.

But say it is night.
Night as in early morning.

Alice awake.

The baby fused
to her breast.

When David stirs
she says

you need a wife
of your own.

Let us pray about it.

Maybe he kneels
and she sits up in bed
holding the baby
as the baby's mouth
holds her.

And Martha sleeps
with her sister
in the other room.

Or
the baby
is big enough to sleep
with his sisters

so their mother
who is forty two
might sleep through the night.

But likely

in this first frontier house

there is only one room.

When David rises

his stepdaughter

Martha

the next

girl

he sees.

Family stories:

Alice suggested Martha
to David
herself.

But here

my imagination

breaks.

The words
won't come
out

of the mother's mouth.

MARTHY

on saturday
mother braids my hair

on wednesday
she lets it down

puts her small bone
comb against my head

pulls me through
her white teeth

she braids her own hair
looking in the bit of tin

her white parts
straight as her seams

she lets me darn his socks
then eyes my thread

unpicks the black hole
and cleans

the mouth shut

II

My Dear Wives & Family ...
kiss the baby for me

—David Wilson Tullis, 1883

my sweet Marthy,

Glasgow is so cold
today my fingers
barely clasp the pen
I hear rain even
in the house when
we go down to break
fast I smell damp earth
beneath each bite
some godly folks here
ripe for gospel I try
I talked with one
woman the spirit
took over me so
I don't know
what I said it started
in my words Testifying
then the Spirit took
and filled
my speaking
she began to cry
would not stop crying
her mother took her
she reminded me of you
eyes lighter blue
more freckle
but be still
the Lord
will bless us
for the sacrifices
you make
I am here
I pray for Mother
and Thomas
each night
then I start over
and pray for you

feel this
even as you are home
and I am here
touch the corner
where I've marked it
I'm touching it too
God is grateful
his saints will be soon

Dear Father

Thomas was sick last week
sweating and crying in bed
as pale as a shell
he is better now
but scared momma
momma hardly spoke
the third night
he was in bed
I don't know if it was spirit
or my mind
but just before
the fever broke
I sat with him
by the fire
I thought
he looked just like papa
for a moment
his nose
a little sharper
otherwise perfect
reflection papa but
sleeping but
a boy like I never
saw him as

you and momma
did the sitting up
when papa got sick
but I remember
the day he died
the morning

I woke early
started the coffee
you came in
from papa's bedside
saw me
boiling coffee
not knowing
papa was dead

your face
when you see me
I mustve been eleven
I thought
you mustve taken
me bare
foot loose haired
starting that little fire
to be a ghost slipped in
through the new glass window

dear

today the baby ate
a little tomato
her first

        the face she made!

I gave her a boiled one too
she likes this better

she is pretty
thin faced

        like you

I worry
about her quiet

            at her age
Thomas could
sing hymns
chase chickens
hold the door

        she doesn't even cry

Momma promises
it'll be a boy
this time

all the salt
I've been wanting

I had the dream again last night

he'll come before the snow

III

I had no saints, so I turned
to my ancestors

—Susan Elizabeth Howe, *Salt*

WORK

my grandmother did not

    sew or cook

        what did she do

she read books

    my mother says

        she read history

IN THE BRIGHAM YOUNG MEMORIAL PARK IN A DROUGHT SUMMER AFTER A DROUGHT SUMMER

Salt Lake City, Utah

a woman tills
the earth
forever her
shoulders never
lift their gentle
bend to soil
the boy
at her feet
prods irrigation water
with his bronze stick

years of some
rain years of
heavy snow
years brushed
these bronze bodies
into green
green bronze
and green still
flexed and bent
the woman
tills earth
forever

& nothing
ever grows

REMEMBRANCE

is different

I know

than remembering

SAINT GEORGE, UTAH

Not named for the Saint
who met the princess by
the lake and with her girdle
leashed the dragon. Who killed it

for the people's conversion.
Whose chapel in Windsor
holds a part of his skull
part of his arm or

his heart. In
a griffin's egg cup
two of his fingers.
Mormons have no saints

save the pioneers. Saint George
after the cousin of Joseph Smith.
George A. Smith who the Paiutes
called *Non-choko-wicher*

takes himself apart after watching
how he removed his teeth
glasses and wig. George did not
settle that place but called

the saints who settled it.
Instructed them to eat
potatoes raw with skin
to prevent scurvy.

They called him Potato Saint.
A few miles north my English
great great grandmother
once ate only potatoes

and salt for three weeks.
Her husband called on a mission
to Europe. There was
no other food.

I do not know
what her sister wife
ate. When her baby
fell into the fire

she rubbed halved
potatoes onto the burned
hands. Wrapped each finger
separately so they would not

graft together.
But cut one finger
three months later
because they said

it was corrupting
the other fingers in.
She told this story
from England.

A poor woman's
pastor visits and asks
to pray with her.
As he prays she

interrupts
him with
potatoes!
potatoes!

When he stops
she explains God
might hear her need
slipped between the man's words

    and send
    the starving woman
    potatoes.
    Potatoes.

This is the joke.

WORK

ancestor dolls were not
dolls we played with
but dolls we made
at church
picking fabrics
with our mothers

                    all mothers sewed
                        a little

          one girl made Pocahontas
          as in Disney
          a distant cousin

I made my namesake
working from mind
rather than picture

royal blue for her dress
egg white apron
I picked auburn yarn
hair auburn the color
I wished for myself

there is no one alive who remembers
the color of her hair

there is no one to correct me

I was eight
the year we made the ancestors

old enough to choose
good from evil

two new dresses
on my baptism
birthday

one dress before
I went under water
one dress after

on Easter we got one dress each

my mother took a picture
me and her daffodils
my father made
the slideshow of my life
burned it onto a CD
and in sharpie made my name

I DREAM

I meet my ancestors.
They are proud of me.

I meet Juanita Brooks,
the Mormon historian

who published
The Mountain Meadows Massacre.

Who expected excommunication for writing it.
Who died six years before I was born.

I am unprepared and ask her only two questions.
One about graves.

But how are they made?

I am deciding whether to marry a high school boyfriend
who is facing life in prison for raping two women
over twenty times.
In the dream
we are in bed.
In my bed I am alone.

He is days away from trial.

I DO NOT KNOW

where my own rapist is.
The high school boyfriend in jail
was more like the friend
who taught me to drive stick
in the church parking lot.
Took me to the homecoming dance,
brought my mother flowers.

REENACTMENT

Martin's Cove, Wyoming

we good
girls pushed
and pulled
handcarts
down one
hill up
another
flour sack
babies on
our hips
long skirts
matching
pale bonnets
we sewed with
our mothers
our mothers
said we
pulled
to honor
the pioneer
women who
pulled after
their men
joined the
Mormon
Battalion
our own
congregation
of boys

waited on
the last
hill wide
brimmed hats
in hands
when we
stopped
pulling
they offered
each girl
a little red
drawstring
bag
its belly
full on
a few
red
pebbles
for who
can find
a virtuous
woman
her price
is far
above
rubies

REENACTMENT

The Mormon Trail, Wyoming

Not everyone had a pioneer ancestor they could claim.
We were being the real handcart company.

But Martha and her family were in that company
that left too late.

For four days,
I was Martha.

Her name in plastic
hung low on my chest
like a medallion.

HYRUM, UTAH

Named after Joseph
Smith's older brother.
Mormonism's
beloved martyrs

shot
by a mob.
Joseph fell
through the jail

window crying
Oh Lord my God.
Half the Masonic
distress call

Oh Lord
my God
is there no hope
for a widow's son?

One year someone
prayed over the fourth
of July parade in Spanish.
Weeks of letters

to the editor.
On blood
boiling days
you could smell

the meat
packing plant
inside the
school bus.

ICE raided the plant
on December twelfth.
The Day of Our Lady
of Guadalupe.

The day the Virgin Mary
asked Juan Diego
Am I not here
I who am your mother?

I DREAM

father won't let
me unkeep the baby

            grandfather digs

                        I have no husband here

WHAT I MISS ABOUT BELIEVING

singing

with

others

FAITH

I do not believe
in ghosts

especially now

when no one
has come for me

when I dream
of my ancestors

they are
strangers

who do not
tell me
the truth

my bible says
to die
is to give up
the ghost

I hesitate
to label it
metaphor

& picture
a kind
of throwing

I feel closer
to Martha

I am
a daughter

          poor at keeping systems
               bad at faith

          still
at Martha's grave
I take a pink
rock
the width
of my finger
tip &
               speak

GILGAL GARDEN

after Thomas Battersby Child Jr.

Salt Lake City, Utah

in the garden of stones   a stone woman watches

nothing to hold

save a quiet translation

sun stone wind

chain link

if I had faith like Child's

stones

I would want that faith

IV

Dear Father ...
Mother seis she cant write to you like she cauld talk ta you
ma seas she is [ ] some times ...

—Martha Jane Tullis on Martha, her mother, to David, her father, 1883

I

pray

over
you

feel

his will soon

a shell
is

a

reflection

the
sick
remember

the

dead

see me

bare
haired

through the window

you

hold

the salt

the snow

V

Being haunted, becoming aware of a presence of a presence ...
The perceiver might be a sieve that experience falls through.

—Elizabeth Robinson, *On Ghosts*

HELPMEET

Say the house was his.
Alice lived there
with her husband
her children
and him.
Her husband died.
Some days it reads
simple as money.

ALICE DREAMS

she is washing Thomas' shirts.
She is beating them on the pink rock.
The angel says
                                        Thomas is dead.

            She will give the shirts to David.
She is washing David's shirts in Little Pinto
where he will baptize her again.

MARTHA DREAMS

her mother's face in the cellar.
Grey eyes closed under a barrel
of yellow pears. The boys are nowhere
when the roof breaks. She opens the yolks
over the fire. Someone has killed
the young rooster. His neck reaches
clear across the yard.

DREAM

Grandma is teaching me to weave birds.
They are black thread birds. When she stops I
slip in my hand to see that they are still
downy. Grandma's mouth is sewn with a
thread the color of her hair. Outside
I gather the red dirt. I will make
a robin from this dirt. I spit
on my hands until the bird breathes.

MORNING SONG

kettle cry

in this house

jacob's ladder

lifted

no angels

comin

up or down

ALICE DREAMS

she cannot find her comb
and the house has no babies
rooms or beds. Only dirt floor
and colored strips someone
cut for quilting. The red cloth
spreads. Her fingers rake
the white strands as if
they belong to someone else.
Someone else
finds the knot and pulls.

MARTHA DREAMS

of green apples. Of Bolton.
Of pissing her only dress
when she couldn't stand
in the boat's black belly.
Of the baby hardening in
her black dress. Her mother
breathes nearby. Her baby
loose in the bed. In her
dreams their husband stands
an inch above the dirt.

THE NEIGHBOR DESCRIBES MARTHA AS

always

in that bedroom

had her family so fast

didn't get out much

meek little lady

didn't say much

first boughten carpet

in Pinto

HELPMEET

do the math
again

I am wrong

the baby came
six months

and thirteen days
after Martha

married
her stepfather

the baby
only eleven months

younger
than her own

half brother
and uncle

her baby
here

the topsoil
a crust

my boot
breaks through

no one suggested
he marry Martha

it was
the solution

I am too
late

[ ]

her basket is full
of mice who wake
run waves over her
when she remembers
lifts the linen and looks

[   ]

she left her temple dress on
the road. Here it is
red with earth.
The girl finds it.
Pulls silk on and walks.

DREAM

Vomit even in my dreams.
Yellow vomit dresses potato beds.
There is no room inside my dress for this.
Mother works the dresses smaller. I feel
it's working through my dreams.
This future is made of mouths.
Mouths closing on my body.

DREAM

<table>
<tr><td>the baby</td><td>eats</td></tr>
<tr><td>snow</td><td>screams</td></tr>
<tr><td>at my nipples</td><td>my fingers</td></tr>
<tr><td>I feed him</td><td>under mittens</td></tr>
<tr><td>ghosts</td><td>grow</td></tr>
</table>

NOTES

Many of these poems imagine into the lives of my Mormon women ancestors, especially Martha Eccles Tullis, my great great great grandmother, and Alice Eccles Hardman Tullis, her mother and sisterwife.

There is little written directly about these women's lives, feelings, or memories. I have found no primary documents they have left behind.

These poems are part of my attempt to picture what I could not picture about their lives.

I wrote from the stories my mother raised me on and found some other family texts on FamilySearch and the Church History Library. Some historical context shared here:

I

"After"

Stories of Mormon pioneers mistreating, fearing, and resenting the indigenous tribes whose land they were settling are common. Because Mormon pioneer's colonial-settler practices negatively affected many traditional food sources for Utah's native tribes, there was a perception that Indians sometimes expected "handouts" from the Mormons. This is the case with this family story, where a Paiute man expected food and was instead attacked by a frightened woman whose husband was away. In a family storytelling context, this story is an example of the bravery and scrappiness of a Mormon pioneer woman.

"Alice"

Information was pulled from an interview between Beth Tullis Syphus and Mary Ann Platt Seegmiller, a Pinto local, on May 26, 1956. Seegmiller was 82 years old.

About Alice, Seegmiller said, "No one could beat her at figures, and she worked the problems all in her head. She handled all the business deals, the trading of the wheat and the potatoes. She saw that the fences were kept up. She tended to everything. Oh, she had a head on her. She made things go."

She described their Pinto house: "…my folks always called it [the house] Sister Eccles place.… a large house made out of grooved lumber and painted white. It had a large front room on one side, then a hall that went straight back to the kitchen, another large front room on the other side that was called Martha's bedroom. Just behind Martha's bedroom was another smaller room that belonged to Sister Eccles [Alice].… The first 'states' carpet, as we called the boughten carpet, that ever came into Pinto was put in Martha's bedroom."

I am uncertain whether the house she described was the first house the David Wilson Tullis and Eccles family lived in together. If this was the original house, it may have been expanded over time.

A copy of this interview can be located in the Church History Library (MS 21357).

"David Dreams"

Martha was a small woman, even in adulthood. Her granddaughter Cora Tullis Gale recalled, "we never saw them [David and Martha] asleep but what she was lying on his arm. He was a big man and Grandma Martha was a little woman and it almost looked like his little girl lying on his arm." Cora also recorded that he called Martha "Marthy."

"Marthy"

Years after writing this poem, I read that Alice had a beautiful round comb from England, which she wore in the back of her hair.

II

David Wilson Tullis' missionary journal and actual mission letters (to and from his family) have been digitized by the Church History Library and can be viewed online (MS 10182).

David generally addressed his letters to "My Dear Wives and Family," and, after Alice's death in July 1883, "My Dear Wife and Family."

The epigraph quotes from David's April 9, 1883 letter, but he frequently sends love to his children and asked after Martha's baby. When he departed for his mission, Martha and David had eight children. Alice and David had Thomas. Martha gave birth in November 1882, three months after he left, to the ninth.

There are several letters from his children, but there are no letters from Martha.

III

"Work"

The first poem titled "Work" is after Lorine Niedecker's "Poet's work."

"St. George, Utah"

This poem rephrases a line from Elizabeth Howe's poem, "Family Trees" (also the epigraph from section I).

Some information about George A. Smith came from the St. George Daughters of Utah Pioneers Museum. The detail about his Paiute nickname came from *Massacre at Mountain Meadows* by Ronald W. Walker, Richard E. Turley, and Glen M. Leonard.

The woman in this poem is not Martha or Alice, but another pioneer ancestor from England who lived nearby in Santa Clara, Utah. Her daughter, like Martha's, fell into the fire and was badly burned.

"I Dream"

Outside of the scope of these poems, but haunting them, is David Wilson Tullis' participation in the horrible Mountain Meadows Massacre. See *Massacre at Mountain Meadows* (above), and *Vengeance is Mine: The Mountain Meadows Massacre and its Aftermath* by Richard E. Turley and Barbara Jones Brown. The claim that Juanita Brooks expected excommunication comes from Levi S. Petersen's *Juanita Brooks: Mormon Woman Historian.*

"Hyrum, Utah"

The closing prayer at Hyrum City's 2010 Fourth of July celebration was given in Spanish. Many locals sent emails and letters to the editor to complain.

ICE raided the meat-packing plant in Hyrum on December 12, 2006.

IV

This epigraph from Martha Jane (Martha and David's daughter) is the closest we get to a direct quote from Martha. The epigraph is transcribed exactly as it appears in the manuscript, except that Martha Jane signs off "Marthe" and I replaced the transcriber's use of "......" with empty brackets. This letter is dated February 5, 1883.

When descendants typed up David's mission diary in the twentieth century, the pages were full of ________, indicating places where text presumably could not be read or information was left out of the transcription. David's pages are full of these gaps.

These poems are erasures from section II.

V

"Helpmeet"
Most family accounts state that Alice, Thomas, and their daughters moved into David's house in Pinto. Some family accounts claim Alice had her own house, and David married and moved in with her. Regardless, it seems that the house was locally referred to as belonging to Alice ("Sister Eccles' house.")

"The Neighbor Describes Martha As"
This is a found poem pulled from an interview between Beth Tullis Syphus and Mary Ann Platt Seegmiller (see above).

"Helpmeet"
At least one family story claims Martha and David were civilly married in Pinto in April 1863 and sealed in Salt Lake City in August 1863. If they were married in April, Alice and David's child (Thomas) was one month old, making Martha fifteen years old when she married her stepfather. If they were married in August, Thomas was five months old, and Martha sixteen years old. I have only found documentation of their sealing date of August 1863. Martha gave birth to her first child, Euphemia, in February 1864. She was sixteen years old.

ACKNOWLEDGMENTS

I am grateful to the following journals for giving many of these poems their first homes (often under other titles): *Sugar House Review, Ghost City Review, Dialogue: A Journal of Mormon Thought, The Ponder Review, Rock & Sling,* and *Up the Staircase Quarterly.*

Thank you to Ghost City Press, who published my micro-chap *Dream With Teeth* in 2023. *Dream With Teeth* included a handful of poems that were composed at the intersection of family stories and fairy tales. I'm excited to see some of these poems reprinted here under different titles.

Thank you to my teachers who believed in and pushed these poems: Jennifer Atkinson, Sally Keith, Peter Streckfus, Susan Tichy, and Eric Pankey. I am so grateful for our conversations. Thank you, always, to my first writing mentor, Jennifer Sinor.

Thank you to the world's greatest MFA cohort: Chris Stanzione, Ana Pugatch, Martin Mitchell, Kell Pieper, Emily Okamoto-Green, Danielle Williams, and Shane Chergosky. Bless you for reading so many dead pioneer poems.

Thank you to my larger George Mason University writing community and the Creative Writing program. Being awarded the 2020–2021 Poetry Thesis Fellowship helped me research and write many of these poems.

Thank you to Dayna Patterson, who offered me and these poems so much support. Thank you especially for your generous example in feminist, post-Mormon poetry. Your book gave me courage to write this one.

I am grateful to Alyssa Quinn for their long friendship and belief in this book. Thank you for coming in at the final hour and making everything better.

I am forever grateful to the Logan writing communities and that shaped me into a writer. Special thanks to Britt Skye, Star Coulbrooke, Shaun Anderson, and all the good folks I met through Ray B. West and Helicon West.

Thank you to the Utah Original Writing Contest for awarding Honorable Mention to an earlier version of this manuscript in 2021.

Thank you to the Sundress Academy of the Arts. Spending time with this project at Firefly Farms was a gift the book needed.

Thank you to the wonderful folks at Signature Books for your wholehearted support of this book.

I am grateful to my family, especially to my mother, who unwittingly made me a writer. Mom, this book would not exist if you did not believe in telling family stories and loving family names. Thank you to my grandparents, who taught her that love.

Thank you to Taylor, who moved away from and back to Utah with me, who listened to me talk and cry about this book, and who cheers for me in all things.

Thank you to the many, many writers whose works have transformed me into a better writer, poet, and person.

I am thankful to the volunteers at the Daughters of Utah Pioneer Museums and those who assisted me at the Church History Library. I am thankful for the gold mine that is FamilySearch. Thank you to the cemeteries in Providence, Logan, Santa Clara, Panaca, Pinto, Panguitch, their visitors, and their caretakers.

Thank you to my many living and dead, especially those who captured/recorded/saved names, pictures, and their versions of stories where I might find them.

ABOUT THE AUTHOR

Millie Tullis is a poet, editor, and researcher from northern Utah. She holds an MFA from George Mason University and an MA in American Studies & Folklore from Utah State University. Her poetry has been published in *Dialogist*, *Sugar House Review*, *Cimarron Review*, *Dialogue*, *Ninth Letter*, and elsewhere. Her digital micro-chapbook, *Dream With Teeth*, was published by Ghost City Press in 2023. Her research has won awards from the Utah Historical Society, the Folklore Society of Utah, and the American Folklore Society. She is the editor-in-chief of *Exponent II*. Find more at millietullis.com.